The
Autism Mom
Cooks
Gluten-Free Casein-Free

# Classic American Cuisine

*The Autism Mom Cooks Gluten-Free Casein-Free Classic American Cuisine*

Copyright ©2009 Stephanie Hemenway

ISBN-10: 1-4392-3481-7
ISBN-13: 9781439234815

Library of Congress Control Number: 2009903048

**All Rights Reserved.**

No part of this publication may be reproduced or transmitted in any form or by any means, electronic or mechanical, including photocopy, digital, recording, or any information storage and retrieval system-except for brief quotations in printed reviews, without prior permission of the author.

**Printed with pride in the United States of America**

# Contents

Introduction .................................. Pg 5

The GF/CF Home ............................ Pg 7

Allergen-free Condiments &
   Ingredients ................................ Pg 17

Snacks ........................................ Pg 21

Breakfast ..................................... Pg 31

Lunch ......................................... Pg 45

Dinner ........................................ Pg 65

Side Dishes .................................. Pg 91

Breads ........................................ Pg 105

Dessert ....................................... Pg 113

Index .......................................... Pg 135

# Introduction

Over the last few years, the advantages of the Gluten-Free Casein-Free (GF/CF) Diet have been well-documented by parents, yet a lot of families still have not tried it, or have been unable to stick with it for any length of time. Invariably, the same two reasons are always given; their kids flat-out won't eat the GF/CF foods they've tried to serve, or the cost of purchasing special GF/CF foods in addition to their weekly groceries is beyond an already "stretched-to-the-breaking-point" household budget.

This cookbook is designed for those families. The recipes here are specially modified versions of familiar classic American foods that most families are already used to eating, so that the whole family can eat the same meals. They taste as good as their non-GF/CF counterparts, and because they are all made from scratch, they cost no more to prepare. In fact, you may actually find that your grocery bills go *down*. These recipes are based on the meals families used to eat in your grandparents' day, back when autism, ADHD, asthma and diabetes were exception rather than the rule.

Cooking from scratch is a lot easier than most people imagine, and takes no more time to prepare than so-called "convenience" foods. Most of the meals in this cookbook can be prepared in around half-an-hour, or about the average length of time it takes to have a pizza delivered.

The recipes you find in this cookbook are not difficult, even for beginner cooks, and the results are well-worth the effort. Give them a try, and let your whole family discover that GF/CF can be a great way to eat!

# The GF/CF Home

Once your family realizes that GF/CF food can taste every bit as good as "regular" food, the easiest and most cost-effective approach is to simply keep a "GF/CF Home", where everything in the house can be eaten by each and every family member.

What about nutrition? Is the GF/CF diet healthy? Many mainstream pediatricians who are unfamiliar with the GF/CF diet worry that it may cause nutritional deficiencies, and this can scare parents away from trying something that may be of great benefit to their child.

Although the GF/CF diet removes all dairy products from the diet, it's important to remember that dairy products are only *one* source of dietary calcium (a cup of collard greens has more calcium than a cup of milk) and protein (meat and eggs both beat dairy products in the protein department) and there are many other flours every bit as nutritious, if not more so, as the wheat flour that we use almost exclusively in this country.

The truth is, much of the world consumes a lot less milk and wheat than we do with no ill effects at all. In fact, they are actually healthier, leaner, and suffer from less chronic disease. Japan, for example, eats a primarily rice-based diet and consumes a lot less milk, and the Japanese boast both the world's lowest infant mortality rate *and* a longer life expectancy than the United States. Odds are, if you follow these recipes (all of which are made from whole fresh ingredients with no chemical additives, preservatives, or artificial flavors and colors) your family will probably be eating much "healthier" than ever before. And if you're still worried about that lack of milk, a natural chewable multivitamin with added calcium can provide peace of mind.

In terms of cost, because these recipes rely on basic ingredients rather than prepackaged or pre-prepared foods, feeding your family based on the recipes in this cookbook will probably *cut* your weekly grocery bill rather than increase it. GF/CF flours may cost more than a plain bag of white flour, but homemade GF/CF cookies are still a lot cheaper than a package of "regular" cookies, and they taste a lot better, too!

You may find that many items in your regular grocery store are in fact GF/CF though they may not be manufactured in what are called "dedicated facilities". A perfect example would be semi-sweet chocolate chips. Ghirardelli® Semi-sweet Morsels (approximately $2-$3 a bag at your local grocery store) are technically GF/CF, although they are made in a factory that also produces milk-based items. As such, there may be trace cross contamination. Cross-contamination is critical when you have an allergy (like shellfish or peanuts) which may produce anaphylaxis, but probably less critical when cooking GF/CF. You will have to decide, based on your family's budget and your child's own food based sensitivities, if the ingredients you buy need to come from GF/CF dedicated facilities.

## Dietary Enzymes

These are natural enzymes that help break down gluten, casein, phenols, and pretty much anything else you can think of. If your child is on a GF/CF diet and in school or daycare (or any situation in which you don't have 100% food control), daily enzymes are a good "insurance policy." Houston Labs' Peptizyme and Klaire Labs' Vitalzymes (Klaire labs products must be ordered through a physician) are two commonly used enzymes.

## Phenols 101

Phenols are substances either occurring naturally in, or added to, many foods, and an excess can negatively affect neurological function in kids. The biggest offenders? *Artificial flavors and colors.* Back in the early 1980s, my little brother was part of the "first wave" of ADD/ADHD kids to start turning up. Rather than putting him on Ritalin®, which was just starting to gain popularity back then, my parents removed all artificial colors and flavors from our house as recommended in the Feingold Diet. It worked far better, and without any of Ritalin's side effects. *Thirty years* after Dr. Ben Feingold's book on the subject was first published, the American Academy of Pediatrics finally admitted that artificial flavors and colors can cause hyperactivity, attention difficulties, and other physical and behavioral problems in children. Checking food labels and rejecting anything with artificial flavors, colors, and/or phenols (this applies to over-the-counter drugs also) in its ingredients list is an inexpensive and simple way to make a huge difference in your child's behavior. None of the recipes in this book include any artificial flavors or colors. (It's worth noting that one of the most common hidden sources of artificial flavors and colors is *toothpaste* – simply switching to all-natural Tom's Toothpaste® can make a big difference. It was the only toothpaste in our house when I was growing up, and we still use it exclusively. It may be entirely coincidental, but my brother and I have virtually no cavities!)

## Corn, Soy and Nuts

Many doctors believe that in addition to GF/CF, certain children with ASD can benefit from the removal of corn, soy and nut based products from their diets. For these children the three potential allergens often cause an inflammatory response. At the end of each recipe you will find instructions for preparing them without corn, soy, or nuts. Those few recipes that cannot be easily modified (like cornbread) can simply be avoided.

## Eggs

Whole eggs are a wonderful source of protein, vitamins and minerals, and essential dietary cholesterol, which is critical for normal neurological development in infants and children. Recent research has shown that many children on the autism spectrum suffer from dangerously low cholesterol levels and can actually benefit from the incorporation of eggs into their diets. The recipes in this cookbook have not been designed to be egg-free.

## Fats

You will find that several of the recipes allow a choice of oil, shortening, or lard. The following is a list of fats used in this book. The recipes have been tested using these oil & shortenings, so if the recipe allows for a choice, you may choose the ones that best suit your family's budget and food-based sensitivities.

**Oils:**

- **Olive oil** - A true classic, and highest in monounsaturated ("good") fat. The lighter olive oils are better for those with phenol sensitivities.
- **Safflower oil**– This oil is inexpensive, clean, and good at high heats.
- **Coconut oil**- A perfect oil for baking & frying, it's used specifically in several recipes. Coconut oil is solid at temperatures below 74° F, but melts easily. It is high in saturated fat, but makes up for that by being soy-free and a good source of monolauric acid, a natural anti-viral compound. As with olive oil, "extra-virgin" has a stronger flavor, so if you are not a real fan of coconut, it's not worth the extra cost. And since the coconut is well-protected from pesticides by its shell, "organic" is probably not so critical here, either. You'll find it next to shortening in your local grocery store.
- **Vegetable oil** - Corn and soy based oils are commonly labeled "vegetable oil" and are very inexpensive. However, the fats they contain may not be as healthy as was once believed, so they should probably be used sparingly unless cost is the primary factor.
- **Bacon grease (used in specific recipes only)** - Odds are unless there were cultural reasons prohibiting it, your mother or grandmother had a jar of bacon drippings in the fridge. It adds wonderful flavor and is a traditional favorite of cooks everywhere. Nutritionally, bacon grease is similar to lard, but with a more "bacony" flavor.

**Shortenings:**

- **Lard** - Southern women rejoice! Lard is back on the "A-list" after years of bad PR. Inexpensive, naturally gluten-free and casein free, lard is low in Omega 6 and high in Omega 3 fatty acids, and is a natural source of selenium, zinc, and Vitamin D. It contains nearly 50% monounsaturated fat, which is higher than flaxseed oil. (All this may help to explain why lard has traditionally been the staple fat of several cultures known for their great longevity, like Cuba and Okinawa.) Hands-down the best fat for frying, lard makes famously flaky pastry and a nice delicate cookie too.
- **Butter flavor Crisco®** - Very inexpensive and providing consistent results in baked goods, Crisco is soy based, which makes it a poor choice for those with soy sensitivities. Highly processed, it is also the least "natural" of the fats used.
- **Palm Shortening** – This is a good shortening for those avoiding soy and corn. It's great for baking and frying and widely available.

## GF Flours

You'll find a full list of GF flours and starches needed to prepare the recipes in this book in the GF/CF Pantry list. If you can afford organic flours, by all means buy them - often, the best prices can be had by ordering by the case at **Amazon.com**. If you're looking for lower-cost alternatives try The Cheese Shop in Stuart's Draft, VA (online at **TheCheeseShopVa.com**.) It is a great source for high quality (though not always organic) GF/CF ingredients, in very basic packaging, with prices often less than half what you'll find anywhere else. A Mennonite-owned business, they carry all the flours you'll need to make the recipes in this cookbook. Please note that not everything in the store may be on the website, so if you are looking for a specific ingredient and can't locate it on the website contact the store directly at (540) 337-4224.

## Organics

Certified Organic food, grown without pesticides and chemical fertilizers, is wonderful. However, you may come across a few obstacles. Availability may be limited - in many rural areas it's still difficult to get a wide variety of organics at reasonable prices. You may want to check and see if there is a whole-foods-cooperative in your area. You can also ask your local grocery store to carry certain items you purchase regularly, or find online markets for non-perishables with low shipping fees (if you order with other moms you may be able to save on shipping.)

Prices for Certified Organic food can be prohibitive so it pays to shop around. Many stores have their own less expensive "house brand" organics. When buying chicken, rather than buying organic free-range (which can easily wipe out a grocery budget), consider "hormone & antibiotic free" instead. Food Lion and Tyson both market this.

## Local Meat and Produce

Buying produce at your local farmers' market is a great way to get fresh food at great prices, while supporting local farmers and reducing the amount of fuel needed to transport it. Even if they are not "certified organic," small farms need to use far less in the way of pesticides than the huge commercial farms, and practice a greener form of agriculture that's good for the planet.

## The Family Garden

The absolutely cheapest way to obtain fresh organic produce is to simply grow it yourself. During WWII every American family dug up part of their lawn and planted a Victory Garden - Eleanor Roosevelt even had one on the White House lawn! It's inexpensive, good exercise and fun for kids. (Children are much more likely to eat vegetables they've grown themselves!) Dig up a sunny chunk of lawn, or pick up some pots and do some container gardening. Tomatoes, lettuce, green beans, and strawberries are great for beginners.

## Wild Game

If you have a hunter in your family, it's worth remembering that "wild" red meats like venison and elk (and wild poultry like pheasant and quail) are about as organic as you can get. The recipes in this book lend themselves very well to wild game so feel free to simply exchange the meat suggested for game of a similar cut and weight.

## A Cheap Alternative

If organic produce is simply not in your family's budget, a $3 bottle of Organic Fruit & Vegetable Wash can help remove pesticides and bacteria from food

## Kitchen Help

Get a step-stool and get your kids to work in the kitchen. Though at first uninterested, my son is now a baking *fanatic*. He slides his step-stool to the counter and sidles up to help as soon as he sees me starting to cook. You can learn together, read recipes, mix, measure, scoop & pour. It's a great opportunity for them to master skills and build confidence. My little guy is also far more inclined to try something new if he helped prepare it.

# Kitchen Items Worth Investing In

Below is a list of inexpensive items no GF/CF kitchen should be without.

- kitchen timer (watching a clock is not really an option for most of us)
- meat thermometer
- candy/deep-fry thermometer
- melon baller - for making cookies
- pastry cutter
- stand or hand held electric mixer
- electric waffle iron (a must if toaster waffles are a family favorite - my Toastmaster® is 12 years old and still makes perfect waffles)
- large cast iron skillet (available at many small hardware stores)
- large cast iron dutch oven (available at many small hardware stores)
- blender that can crush ice cubes
- Rival® gel canister ice cream maker (uses no ice or salt)
- electric griddle
- Westbend Stir Crazy® Corn Popper (available at amazon.com)
- Frydaddy® (available at amazon.com)
- food dehydrator (great if your kids loves dried fruit or fruit rollups - fast & so much less expensive with no preservatives)
- 2 glass bread pans (4.5 x 8.5")
- freezer bags, parchment paper, wax paper, tin foil and pint/quart size mason jars with plastic lids.

# The GF/CF Pantry

The items listed in the GF/CF Pantry, Fridge & Freezer will allow you to make all of the recipes in this cookbook.

arrowroot starch/flour*
baking powder*
baking soda*
Basic Flour Mix :
    2 cups tapioca starch
    2 cups potato starch
    2 cups arrowroot flour
(Sift together & store in airtight container)
brown rice pasta* (Note: lowest prices I've found are at Wal-mart & vitacost.com)
canned pineapple rings
cocoa powder*
coconut milk
coconut oil
Corn Chex®
cream of tartar*
cream soda
crispy brown rice cereal*
dried fruit*
Egg Replacer (Ener-G®)*
GF/CF semi-sweet chocolate chips
GF/CF vanilla extract* (Rodelle Organic® is available at many chain grocery stores)
lard
peanut butter (Sunbutter® if sensitive)
potato starch (not flour)*
powdered sugar*
Rice Chex®
salt*
shortening
spices*
sweet white sorghum flour*
tapioca starch/flour*
Real Lime® powder 2.85oz shaker (not individual packets as they contain casein)
unflavored gelatin*
vegetable oil of choice
white rice flour (not sweet)*
white vinegar (if corn sensitive-use apple cider vinegar
xantham gum*  (guar gum can replace xantham in recipes if extremely sensitive to xantham - though results will be slightly different)

* indicates flours & baking supplies that can be purchased on discount at TheCheeseShopVa.com

## The GF/CF fridge

- eggs (large)
- rice milk
- hotdogs (low/no nitrates)
- ham (low nitrates)
- fresh fruit
- fresh vegetables
- baking yeast*
- nutritional yeast*
- condiments
- bacon grease
- Lea & Perrins® Worcestershire Sauce (or corn-free GF/CF alternative)

## The GF/CF freezer

- whole chicken
- boneless/skinless chicken
- ground beef
- beef stew meat
- tater tots
- carrots
- peas
- mixed vegetables
- green beans
- mixed peas & carrots
- juice concentrate

## Grocery Store Treats

- potato chips
- plain tortilla chips
- corn chips
- GF/CF pretzels*
- nuts*
- potato crisps
- sweet potato chips
- plantain chips
- fruit leather (avoid artificial colors/flavors)
- dark & semisweet chocolate (check for casein)
- Yummy Earth® lollypops & hard candy
- Surf sweets® jelly beans & gummies
- junior mints (check labels)
- Jelly Belly® naturals jelly beans
- Gummy candy (try: Haribo® (happy cola), TIP®, Trolli® check labels for artificial colors/flavors.
- Coca-Cola Classic®
- lemon lime soda (natural colors/flavors)
- ginger-ale (no artificial colors)
- root beer (no artificial colors)
- mini meringues (check labels)
- Wholefruit® frozen fruit bars with no artificial colors/flavors

**Note:** if avoiding corn look for soda made with cane sugar (Jones® is available at most grocery stores and Coca Cola makes a corn-free Kosher Coca-Cola Classic®

# Allergen-free Condiments & Ingredients

## Corn-free Syrup

**prep: 5 min.**
**cook: 15 min.**

*Replaces corn syrup in recipes

### Ingredients:

2 cups sugar
3/4 cup water
1/4 teaspoon cream of tartar
pinch of salt (optional)

Makes 2 cups

### Method:

1. Combine all ingredients in saucepan.
2. Bring to boil over medium heat, stirring constantly.
3. Reduce heat to low, continue stirring and simmer until reaches softball stage (forms into pliable ball when dropped in cold water. (240°F on candy thermometer)
4. Cool & store in sealed jar in cool dry location for up to 2 months.

## Corn-free Baking Powder

**prep: 5 min.**

### Ingredients:

1/8 cup tapioca starch
1/8 cup baking soda
1/4 cup cream of tartar

### Method:

1. Combine all ingredients in glass jar and shake well.
2. Store in sealed jar in cool dry place.

## Classic American Ketchup

prep: 5 min.
cook: 20 min.

### Ingredients:

1 can tomato paste (6oz)
1/2 cup corn-free syrup
1/2 cup cider vinegar
1/4 water
1 tablespoon sugar
1 teaspoon salt
1/4 teaspoon onion powder
dash of garlic powder

### Method:

1. Combine all ingredients in saucepan.
2. Whisk until smooth bring to boil over medium heat.
3. Reduce heat to low and simmer, stirring frequently for 20 minutes.
4. Remove from heat and cover until cool.

Store in sealed jar in refrigerator.
Makes 2 cups

## Basic Mayonnaise

prep: 10 min.

### Ingredients:

2 egg yolks
1/8 teaspoon salt
1 1/2 cups oil (olive or vegetable oil)
1 tablespoon lemon juice
1 teaspoon Dijon mustard (optional)
salt and pepper to taste

### Method:

1. In a large mixing bowl whisk together the egg yolks and salt.
2. Mixing constantly with electric mixer on medium speed, add oil - **one drop at a time** to the egg yolks until the mixture begins to blend together and thicken.
3. When approximately one quarter of the oil has been incorporated, add the lemon juice and beat into the mixture.
4. Slowly drizzle the remaining oil into bowl in a thin stream while you continue to beat with electric mixer.
5. Once all the oil has been beaten in, add mustard, salt and pepper to taste. Chill mayonnaise in the refrigerator before serving.

Store in sealed jar in refrigerator for 3-4 days.

## Thousand Island Dressing

**prep: 5 min.**

**Ingredients:**

1 cup mayonnaise
2 tablespoons ketchup
1 tablespoon corn-free sweet relish
   or diced sweet pickles
1/4 teaspoon cider vinegar
dash ground paprika (optional)

**Method:**

1. Combine all ingredients.
2. Store in sealed jar in refrigerator.

## BBQ Sauce

**prep: 5 min.**

**Ingredients:**

1 1/2 cups ketchup
1 tablespoon molasses
1 tablespoon honey
2 teaspoons cider vinegar
1/2 teaspoon garlic powder
salt to taste
pepper to taste
dash ground cayenne pepper (optional)

**Method:**

1. Whisk together all ingredients until smooth.
2. Store in sealed jar in refrigerator.

# Snacks

## Classic Snack Mix

**prep:** 5 min.
**cook:** 1 1/2 hours

### Ingredients:

9 cups Rice Chex® cereal
1 cup GF/CF potato crisps
1/2 cup nuts
1 cup GF/CF pretzels
6 tablespoons vegetable oil
2 tablespoons Lea & Perrins Worcestershire sauce
1 teaspoon salt
3/4 teaspoon garlic powder

### Method:

1. Preheat oven to 200°F.
2. Combine cereal, crisps, pretzels & nuts in large bowl.
3. In small bowl mix remaining ingredients.
4. Drizzle over cereal mix, stirring carefully to coat evenly.
5. Place in oven proof pan and bake 1 1/2 hours, stirring occasionally.

**Store in airtight container.**

## Sweet-n-Spicy Snack Mix

**prep:** 5 min.
**cook:** 1 1/2 hours

### Ingredients:

9 cups Rice Chex® cereal
1 cup raisins
1/2 cup nuts
1 cup dried apples
1/2 cup crystallized ginger
1/2 cup coconut oil
1/2 cup sugar
1 1/2 teaspoons cinnamon
1/2 teaspoon ground ginger

### Method:

1. Preheat oven to 200°F.
2. Combine cereal, fruit & nuts in large bowl.
3. In small bowl melt coconut oil in microwave.
4. In separate bowl mix remaining ingredients.
5. Drizzle oil over cereal mix, stir carefully to coat evenly.
6. Sprinkle cinnamon sugar mixture over cereal & stir.
7. Place in oven proof pan and bake 1 1/2 hours, stirring occasionally.

**Store in airtight container.**

**Corn Free:** Rice Chex® may contain trace amounts of corn—replace with rice square cereal of choice; use corn free Worcestershire sauce or omit.
**Soy Free:** use soy free GF/CF pretzels & potato crisps
**Nut Free:** omit nuts

## Juice Gelatin

**prep: 5 min.**
**chill: 4-6 hours**

### Ingredients:

1 envelope unflavored gelatin
1/2 cup cold juice
1 1/2 cups juice (boiling)
1 tablespoon sugar or honey

### Method:

1. In heatproof bowl, sprinkle gelatin onto cold juice. Let sit 1 minute.
2. Add hot juice and stir until gelatin is dissolved.
3. Chill until firm.

To add fruit: chill until soft set then mix in 1 cup fruit and chill until firm (do not use pineapple or kiwi as they will keep gelatin from setting.)

**Makes 4 - 1/2 cup servings**

## Gelatin Blocks

**prep: 5 min.**
**chill: 3-4 hours**

### Ingredients:

4 envelopes unflavored gelatin
1 cup cold fruit juice
3 cups fruit juice, heated to boiling
2 tablespoons sugar or honey

### Method:

1. Sprinkle gelatin over 1 cup cold juice in large bowl and let stand 1 minute to dissolve.
2. Add hot juice & stir until completely dissolved (about 3 minutes.)
3. Stir in sugar or honey
4. Pour into 13 x 9" pan & chill until firm (3-4 hours.) Cut into 1" squares.

**Makes 8-9 dozen blocks**

Corn Free: these recipes are corn-free
Soy Free: these recipes are soy free
Nut Free: these recipes are nut-free

# Traditional Popcorn

**prep: 5 min.**
**cook: 5 min.**

## Ingredients:

1/2 cup popping corn
1-2 tablespoons oil of choice
salt to taste

## Method:

Based on use of West Bend Stir Crazy® (follow manufacturers instructions for different poppers.)

1. Plug in popcorn maker and pour oil onto cooking surface.
2. Add popcorn and cover with lid.
3. Unplug or turn off popper when pops become infrequent.
4. Sprinkle with salt or one of the following seasoning mixes to taste.

**Serves 4**

## Italian Parmesan Seasonings

1/2 teaspoon basil
1/2 teaspoon oregano
(or 1 teaspoon Italian seasoning blend)
1 teaspoon salt
2 tablespoons nutritional yeast
1/4 teaspoon garlic powder

1. Place ingredients in jar, shake to mix.
2. Prepare popcorn using extra virgin olive oil. (optional)
3. Sprinkle seasonings over fresh popcorn taste.

Store any extra well sealed in a cool dry place.

## Tex-Mex Seasonings

1/2 teaspoon ground cumin
3/4 teaspoon chili powder
1/4 teaspoon garlic powder
1 teaspoon salt
1/2 teaspoon True Lime® powder
ground pepper to taste

1. Place ingredients in jar, shake to mix.
2. Prepare popcorn using pepper infused oil. (optional)
3. Sprinkle seasonings over fresh popcorn taste.

Store any extra well sealed in a cool dry place.

Corn Free: N/A
Soy Free: do not use soy based oil
Nut Free: do not use nut based oil

# Nachos

**prep: 10-15 min.**
**cook: 8 min.**

## Ingredients:

1 bag restaurant style tortilla chips
1 cup leftover chili (pg 74) or taco filling (pg76)
1 1/2 cups shredded lettuce
3/4 cup dices tomatoes
1/3 cup diced onion
1/4 cup jalapeño slices (optional)
1/4 sliced black olives
1/2 cup salsa (optional)

### Nacho Cheezy Sauce
2 tablespoons oil
3 tablespoons tapioca starch
2 cups rice milk
1/3 cup nutritional yeast
1 teaspoon lemon juice
1 tablespoon sesame tahini
1 teaspoon salt
1/2 teaspoon garlic powder
1/4 teaspoon chili powder
1/4 teaspoon ground cumin
1/2 teaspoon paprika (for color)

### Guacamole
2 ripe avocados
1/4 teaspoon chili powder
1/4 teaspoon ground cumin
1/4 cup lime juice (1/2 of a fresh lime)
1/4 teaspoon salt
1/4 cup diced onions
1/4 cup dices tomatoes

## Method:

1. Cut up vegetables and set aside

### Nacho Cheezy Sauce
1. In medium saucepan heat oil over medium/low heat.
2. Add tapioca flour and whisk until smooth. Cook until begins boil., stirring often. Reduce heat to low and simmer until flour begins to turn golden 3-5 minutes.
3. Add rice milk and whisk to mix
4. Add all remaining cheese sauce ingredients and simmer 3-4 minutes until thick. Remove from heat and cover.

### Guacamole
1. Peel & remove seeds of avocados.
2. Place in small bowl and mash with fork or potato masher.
3. Add remaining ingredients and mix well. Cover with plastic wrap and set aside.

### Nachos
1. Reheat chili or taco meat in microwave.
2. Place tortilla chips on large serving plate
3. Stir hot Cheezy sauce and pour desired amount over nachos.
4. Put hot chili or taco meat on top and sprinkle with vegetables.

**Serve with guacamole, salsa and remaining Nacho Cheezy sauce.**

**Serves 4**

Corn Free: use corn-free brown rice tortilla chips or baked brown rice tortillas in place of the corn tortillas
Soy Free: ensure chips are not produced with soy based oil
Nut Free: this recipe is nut free

*Breakfast*

## Pancakes

**prep:** 5 min.
**cook:** 6-8 min.

### Ingredients:

**Dry**
1 cup rice flour
1/2 cup tapioca starch
1/4 cup sorghum flour
1/4 cup almond meal
1 teaspoon xantham gum
2 tablespoons sugar
2 teaspoons baking powder
1/2 teaspoon salt
1 teaspoon soda
1 teaspoon egg replacer

**Wet**
2 eggs
2 cups rice milk
2 tablespoons oil
2 teaspoons GF/CF Vanilla

**Additional:**
1/2 to 1 cup water or rice milk for thinning batter as needed.

### Method:

1. Preheat griddle to 350°F (electric) or medium heat on stovetop.
2. Mix dry ingredients until well incorporated.
3. In separate bowl whisk eggs and remaining wet ingredients
4. Add wet ingredients to dry and mix well. Let stand 1-2 minutes to thicken.
5. Ladle batter onto hot griddle and cook until underside is golden and top edges begin to look dry. Carefully flip pancakes and cook until other side is golden.
6. Repeat cooking process. Thin batter as needed with water or rice milk.

**Makes ten 4" pancakes.** Recipe doubles easily for a crowd or freezing cooked pancakes.

**For blueberry pancakes:** gently fold 1 cup washed fresh or frozen blueberries into batter.

## Apple Compote

### Ingredients:

2 tablespoons sugar
1/2 teaspoon cinnamon
1 teaspoon tapioca starch
2 large apples, peeled & sliced
1/2 cup water

### Method:

1. In small saucepan combine sugar, cinnamon & tapioca starch. Add water and apples.
2. Stirring occasionally, cook over low heat until apples are tender and sauce thickens (about 3 minutes.) Add a few additional tablespoons of water if sauce becomes too thick.

---

Corn Free: use corn-free baking powder.
Soy Free: do not use soy based oil.
Nut Free: use 2 tablespoons tapioca starch in place of almond meal

# Waffles

**prep:** 5 min.
**cook:** 15-20 min.

## Ingredients:

**Dry**
1 cup rice flour
2/3 cup tapioca starch
1/3 cup almond meal
1 teaspoon xantham gum
1 tablespoon sugar
3 1/2 teaspoons baking powder
1/2 teaspoon salt
1/2 teaspoon soda

**Wet**
2 eggs
2 cup rice milk
1/3 cup oil
2 teaspoons GF/CF Vanilla

**Additional:**
1/2 cup water or rice milk for thinning batter as needed.

## Method:

1. Preheat waffle iron.
2. Mix dry ingredients until well incorporated.
3. In separate bowl beat eggs and stir in remaining wet ingredients.
4. Add wet ingredients to dry and mix well.
5. Spray waffle iron with cooking spray.
6. Ladle batter (approximately 1/2 cup for a 7" waffle iron) onto waffle iron and close. Cook until golden brown.
7. Repeat cooking process. Thin batter as needed with water or rice milk.

**Makes five 7" waffles.**
Recipe doubles easily for a crowd.

### Time Saver Tip
Double recipe, cool waffles on wire rack and freeze for perfect toaster waffles.

Corn Free: use corn-free baking powder.
Soy Free: do not use soy based oil.
Nut Free: use 1/8 cup sorghum flour in place of almond meal

# French Toast

**prep: 5 min.**
**cook: 15-20 min.**

## Ingredients:

6 slices White Sandwich Bread (pg 106)
3 eggs
1 1/2 cups rice milk
1 teaspoon GF/CF vanilla extract
1/4 teaspoon cinnamon (optional)

spray oil for griddle

## Method:

1. Preheat griddle to 325 - 350°F or medium/low on stovetop.
2. In shallow pan whisk eggs until fluffy, add milk, vanilla and cinnamon and mix well.
3. Cut bread slices diagonally and set in egg mixture.
4. When first side is soaked turn bread over and soak other side.
5. Lightly spray griddle with oil
6. Remove bread from egg mixture and place on hot griddle.
7. When golden flip over and cook until both sides are golden brown and cooked through.

**Serve with real maple syrup or honey.**

**Serves 4**

Corn Free: this recipe is corn free
Soy Free: this recipe is soy free
Nut Free: prepare White Sandwich Bread (pg106) using nut free instructions.

# Oven Omelet

**prep: 5 min.**
**cook: 15 min.**

### Ingredients:

2 tablespoons oil
spray oil
6 mushrooms (washed and sliced)
1 cup fresh spinach (washed and
    chopped into large pieces
1/4 cup diced onion (1 small onion)
4 slices cooked bacon (chopped)
8 eggs
1/2 cup rice milk
1/4 teaspoon salt
dash of pepper

### Method:

1. Preheat oven to 350°F.
2. Oil large cast iron skillet and set aside.
3. Spray medium frying pan with oil and stirring occasionally, cook mushrooms and onions over medium heat until they begin to soften.
4. Add spinach and continue cooking, stirring occasionally, until dark green (about 1 minute.) Remove from heat.
5. In large bowl whisk together remaining ingredients.
6. Heat cast iron skillet over medium heat until edges are hot.
7. Add egg mixture, cook 1 minute stirring occasionally from the bottom of the pan up.
8. Add vegetables and bacon and stir well. Cook 1 minute and remove from heat.
9. Place cast iron skillet in preheated oven and bake until eggs are set (5 - 10 min.)

**Cut into wedges to serve.**

**Serves 4**

### Time Saver Tip

Cook bacon in microwave - place on paper towel draped plate and cook on high for approximately 1 minute per slice.

Corn Free: this recipe is corn free
Soy Free: this recipe is soy free
Nut Free: this recipe is nut free

## Breakfast Scramble

**prep:** 5 min.
**cook:** 8 min.

### Ingredients:

1 cup diced ham
1 cup diced tomato
1/4 cup diced onion
1/2 cup slice mushrooms
6 eggs
1/3 cup rice milk
dash of salt & pepper to taste
cooking spray or 2 teaspoons oil

### Method:

1. Oil small skillet. Cook ham over medium heat until warm (about 2 minutes.)
2. Add vegetable to ham and cook 2 minutes longer. Remove from heat & cover to keep warm.
3. Whisk together eggs, milk, salt & pepper.
4. Oil large skillet and warm over medium heat. When pan is hot add egg mixture. Stir as eggs set, scraping bottom of skillet, repeat until eggs are approximately half cooked (2 minutes.) Add ham and vegetables and cook until eggs reach desired consistency.

**Serves 4**

## Hash Browns

**prep:** 5 min.
**cook:** 10 min.

### Ingredients:

4 medium potatoes
4 tablespoons oil
1/4 teaspoon salt
1/8 teaspoon pepper

### Method:

1. Wash potatoes, poke 2-3 holes in each, set on microwave safe plate & microwave on high for 5 minutes..
2. Hold potatoes with oven-mitt and grate over bowl.
3. Heat oil in cast iron skillet over medium, heat until a drop of water skitters on oil.
4. Gently form shredded potatoes into serving size patties (1/2 cup) and place in oil. Sprinkle with salt and pepper.
5. Cook until golden, then gently turn and cook other side.

**Serves 4**

Corn Free: this recipe is corn free
Soy Free: this recipe is soy free
Nut Free: this recipe is nut free

# Biscuits & Gravy

prep: 5 min.
cook: 10 min.

## Ingredients:

### Biscuits
see pg 108

### Sausage Gravy
1 lb of pork breakfast sausage
4 cups rice milk
3 tablespoons tapioca flour
1/4 teaspoon cracked pepper
1/2 teaspoon salt (or to taste)

## Method:

Prepare biscuits dough and place in oven to bake just prior to preparing gravy.

1. Cook sausage in large cast iron skillet over medium/high heat. Breaking up sausage as it cooks.
2. When sausage is cooked through turn off heat. Remove sausage from pan and set aside.
3. Retain approximately 2-3 tablespoons sausage drippings in the skillet and discard any remaining grease.
4. Heat drippings over medium/low heat. Add tapioca flour and stirring constantly cook for 1-2 minutes.
5. Add rice milk, sausage, salt and pepper. Increase heat to medium. Bring gravy to a boil then reduce heat to low and simmer until desired thickness (5-7 min.)

**Serves 4**

---

Corn Free: ensure sausage does not contain corn syrup
Soy Free: this recipe is soy free
Nut Free: prepare biscuits using nut-free instructions

*Lunch*

# Chicken Noodle Soup

**prep: 10 min.**
**cook: 20 min.**

### Ingredients:

2 tablespoons oil
1.5 lbs boneless skinless chicken cut into small cubes
1 medium onion chopped
5 stalks celery chopped
10 cups chicken broth or stock
2 cups sliced carrots (fresh or frozen)
1 teaspoon salt
1/4 teaspoon garlic powder
1/4 teaspoon ground pepper
1 teaspoon tarragon
2 cups brown rice pasta

### Method:

1. Heat oil in large pot over medium heat.
2. Add chicken, celery and onions. Cook, stirring often until chicken's exterior is cooked and onions begin to look translucent (about 5 min.)
3. Add broth, carrots and spices. Bring to slow boil.
4. Add pasta, stir well and reduce heat to simmer. Simmer until carrots and pasta are both tender (approximately 10-15 min.)

**Serves 4**

### Time Saver Tip
Use 2-3 cups cubed cooked chicken in place of raw. Combine all ingredients except pasta & bring to slow boil. Continue with method # 4.

Corn Free: this recipe is corn free
Soy Free: this recipe is soy free
Nut Free: this recipe is nut free

## Classic Tomato Soup

prep: 5 min.
cook: 5 min.

### Ingredients:

1 tablespoon tapioca flour
1/3 cup cold water
1 (6oz) can tomato paste
2 cups cold water
1/2 teaspoon sugar
1/2 teaspoon salt

### Method:

1. In large saucepan whisk tapioca and 1/3 cup cold water until completely dissolved.
2. Add remaining ingredients. Turn heat to medium and whisk until smooth
3. Cook, stirring often, until edges bubble. Reduce heat to low and continue cooking 1-2 minutes until hot throughout and perfect consistency.

Serves 2

## Grilled Cheezy Sandwiches

prep: 5 min.
cook: 7-9 min.

### Ingredients:

**Cheezy Spread**
2 1/2 tablespoons oil
2 tablespoons rice flour
2 tablespoons tapioca flour
1 cup rice milk
4 tablespoons nutritional yeast
1 1/2 teaspoons salt
1 tablespoon lemon juice
1 tablespoon sesame tahini
1/4 teaspoon finely ground paprika

*or*

**Casein-free Rice American Slices**

2 slices white sandwich bread (pg 106) per sandwich
Oil spray

### Method:

1. Heat oil in small saucepan over low heat. Add flours and whisk together until smooth.
2. Cook, whisking constantly, until mixture begins to turn golden (2-3 min..)
3. Add rice milk and mix well. Add remaining ingredients and bring to boil.
4. Cook, stirring often with whisk, until thick (3-5 min.) Cool slightly and pour into a jar with lid.
5. Spread Cheezy spread on slice of GF/CF bread. Cover with additional slice, brush or spray sandwich exterior lightly with oil and cook in skillet over medium/low heat until golden on both sides. Repeat for each additional sandwich.

Refrigerate any remaining Cheezy Spread in a sealed jar.

Corn Free: this recipe is corn free
Soy Free: this recipe is soy free
Nut Free: this recipe is nut free

# Vegetable Beef Soup

**prep: 10 min.**
**cook: 20 min.**

## Ingredients:

2 tablespoons oil
3/4 cup chopped onion
3 stalks celery (chopped)
1/2 to 1 lb beef (cut into small pieces)
2 tablespoons tapioca starch
8 cups beef broth
1 (28oz) can diced tomatoes (do not drain)
2 cups frozen peas & carrots
3 small potatoes (chopped)
1 cup diced zucchini (optional)
1 cup chopped green beans (frozen or fresh)
1/2 teaspoon garlic powder
2 bay leaves (optional)
salt & pepper to taste

## Method:

1. Heat oil in large pot over medium heat.
2. Add onions & celery. Cook, stirring occasionally.
3. While cooking onions & celery, place beef in plastic bag. Add tapioca and shake well to coat.
4. Add beef to onions and celery. Cook until beef is well browned.
5. Add remaining ingredients and stir well.
6. Bring to slow boil. Then reduce heat to low and simmer until vegetables are tender.

**Serves 4**

Corn Free: this recipe is corn free
Soy Free: this recipe is soy free
Nut Free: this recipe is nut free

# Franks & Beans

**prep: 5 min.**
**cook: 10 min.**

## Ingredients:

1 tablespoon tapioca flour
1 cup cold water
3 (15oz) cans pinto beans (drained)
1/4 cup sugar
1 tablespoon vinegar
1 tablespoon molasses
1 teaspoon salt
1/4 teaspoon ground cloves
1/8 teaspoon pepper
dash pepper sauce (optional)
1 package hot dogs (cut into pieces)

## Method:

1. In medium saucepan, mix tapioca with water until dissolved.
2. Add remaining ingredients and mix well.
3. Over low/medium heat bring to slow boil. Reduce heat to low and simmer 3-4 minutes until sauce thickens and hot dogs are cooked through.

**Serves 4**

Corn Free: this recipe is corn free
Soy Free: this recipe is soy free
Nut Free: this recipe is nut free

# Sloppy Joes

**prep: 5 min.**
**cook: 12 min.**

## Ingredients:

1lb ground beef
1/2 cup diced onion (1 medium)
1/3 cup ketchup
1/4 cup Lea & Perrins® Worcestershire sauce
1 teaspoon salt
1 tablespoon molasses
dash ground pepper to taste
1 teaspoon pepper sauce (optional)

## Method:

1. Heat cast iron skillet over medium heat. Add beef and onions - cook until beef is browned and onions are opaque.
2. Reduce heat to low and stir in remaining ingredients.
3. Cover and cook for 8-10 minutes stirring occasionally.
4. Serve on toasted rolls (pg 106.)

**Serves 4**

Corn Free: use corn-free worcestershire sauce or replace with 1/4 cup BBQ sauce and 1 tablespoon water
Soy Free: this recipe is soy free
Nut Free: prepare rolls using nut free instructions

# Corn Dogs

**prep:** 10 min.
**cook:** 5-7 min.

## Ingredients:

lard or oil for frying

**Dry**
1/2 cup rice flour
1/2 cup tapioca starch
1/4 cup almond meal
2 tablespoons yellow corn meal
1 1/2 teaspoon xantham gum
2 teaspoons baking powder
1/2 teaspoon baking soda
1/2 teaspoon salt

**Wet**
1 1/2 tablespoon oil
1 cup rice milk
2 tablespoons honey
2 eggs beaten

package hot dogs
water for thinning batter if needed

## Method:

*Do not prepare when children are in the immediate area due to the use of hot oil.*

1. Heat oil in deep fryer per manufacturers instructions or 3' deep in a dutch oven over medium heat (bring oil to 365°F.)
2. Rinse and pat dry hot dogs - set aside.
3. Combine all dry ingredients.
4. In separate bowl whisk together wet ingredients then add to the dry ingredients. Mix well.
5. Dip hot dogs in batter (thinning batter as needed with water) and place carefully in oil. Cook until golden on one side then roll to cook other side until both sides are golden brown (5-7min.)
6. While first corn dogs are cooking line a plate with paper towels so hot corn dogs can drain briefly when they are removed from the oil.
7. Insert stick into one end of corn dog if desired and serve.

**Serves 4**

### Time Saver Tip

Increase hotdogs to 2 packages and place any that don't get eaten on a metal rack to cool. Place in freezer bags and freeze for up to 3 months. Reheat for 8-12 minutes on cookie sheet in a preheated 400°F F oven.

Corn Free: omit corn meal
Soy Free: this recipe is soy free
Nut Free: replace almond meal with 2 tablespoons sorghum flour

# Quick-n-Easy Pan Seared Chicken

**prep: 5 min.**
**cook: 10 min.**

## Ingredients:

cooking spray
1 1/2 lbs boneless, skinless chicken (cut into 2" wide strips)
1/2 teaspoon salt
1/8 teaspoon garlic powder
1/8 teaspoon ground pepper
2 tablespoons oil

## Method:

1. Rinse chicken and pat dry.
2. Spray with cooking spray and sprinkle with half of the seasonings. Flip chicken over and repeat process.
3. Heat oil in cast iron skillet over medium heat. When oil is hot carefully place chicken in pan.
4. Cook approximately 5 minutes checking occasionally, turn chicken when surface is golden brown and cook alternate side until it is golden and no longer pink in the center.

**Serves 2 - 4**

**Time Saver Tip**
Refrigerate any leftovers and use for chicken salad (pg 58)

Corn Free: this recipe is corn free
Soy Free: this recipe is soy free
Nut Free: this recipe is nut free

# Mac-n-Cheez

**prep: 5 min.**
**cook: 20 min.**

## Ingredients:

12oz package brown rice elbow macaroni
4 tablespoons oil
2 tablespoons rice flour
2 tablespoons tapioca starch
2 1/2 cups rice milk
4 1/2 tablespoons nutritional yeast
1 1/2 teaspoons salt
1/4 teaspoon garlic powder
1/8 teaspoon mustard
1 tablespoon lemon juice
1 tablespoon sesame tahini
1 teaspoon finely ground paprika

## Crumb topping (optional)

2 slices dry White Sandwich Bread (pg 106)
1 teaspoon nutritional yeast
1/4 teaspoon salt
1 1/2 tablespoons oil

## Method:

Prepare macaroni on stovetop per the manufacturers instructions. As macaroni cooks prepare sauce.

1. Heat oil in medium saucepan over low heat.
2. Whisk in rice flour and tapioca starch. Cook over low heat stirring constantly until sauce begins to turn golden (about 3 minutes.) Add rice milk and whisk until smooth.
3. Add remaining ingredients. Bring to slow boil over low heat, stirring often. Allow to simmer, stirring often, until thick and creamy (5-6 minutes.)
4. Remove from heat and cover to keep warm.
5. When past is cooked (tender but still firm) drain. Do not rinse.
6. Mix pasta and sauce together. Serve immediately or place in ovenproof casserole dish and sprinkle with crumb topping and bake at 400°F until top is golden.

### Crumb Topping
Grate bread into small bowl add remaining ingredients and mix well.

**Serves 4**

Corn Free: this recipe is corn free
Soy Free: this recipe is soy free
Nut Free: prepare White Sandwich Bread (pg 106) for crumbs using nut free instructions.

# Chicken Salad

**prep:** 10 min.
**chill:** 20 min. (optional)

## Ingredients:

1/2 cup GF/CF Mayonnaise
1 tablespoon lemon juice
1 teaspoon salt
1/8 teaspoon ground pepper
1 teaspoon fresh tarragon (optional)
2 cups chopped cooked chicken
1 cup chopped celery (5 stalks)
1/4 cup diced onions (optional)
1/4 cup slivered almonds
1/2 cup quartered seedless grapes

## Method:

1. In small bowl combine mayonnaise, lemon juice, salt, pepper and tarragon.
2. In large bowl combine remaining ingredients. Add mayonnaise mixture and stir until well incorporated.
3. Refrigerate until chilled.

**Serves 4**

---

Corn Free: use corn-free GF/CF mayonnaise.
Soy Free: this recipe is soy free
Nut Free: omit slivered almonds

# Dinner

# Chicken Pot Pie

**prep:** 15 min.
**cook:** 35 min.

## Ingredients:

### Filling
1/4 cup oil
1/3 cup + 2 heaping tablespoons Basic Flour Mix
1/3 cup chopped onion
4 stalks celery (chopped)
1/2 teaspoon salt
1/4 teaspoon ground pepper
1 3/4 cups chicken broth
2/3 cup rice milk
3 cups cooked chicken (cut into 1" pieces)
1 (10oz) package frozen mixed peas and carrots

### Crust
biscuit recipe (pg 108)
potato starch for rolling
wax paper

1 egg beaten
2 tablespoons water

## Method:

1. Heat oil in large saucepan over medium/low heat.
2. Stir in Basic Flour Mix, onion, celery, salt and pepper. Cook for 2-3 minutes, stirring constantly.
3. Slowly stir in broth and rice milk. Bring mixture to a slow boil. Stirring often - boil for 1 minute.
4. Add chicken and vegetables. Stir well and remove from heat. Cover to keep warm.
5. Prepare biscuit dough (pg 108) and set aside.
6. Preheat oven to 425°F.
7. Sprinkle wax paper with potato starch and place biscuit dough on top. Using a rolling pin dusted with potato starch roll dough to 1/2" thick.
8. Pour filling into oven proof casserole and place on cookie sheet with raised edge (to contain any drips while cooking.)
9. Carefully pick up wax paper and invert over casserole, placing crust on top of pot pie. Peel off wax paper and discard.
10. Using a sharp knife cut several slits in the crust to allow steam to escape and flute edges if desired.
11. Mix beaten egg with water and using a basting brush, lightly brush a thin coat of egg wash over the crust.
12. Place in oven and bake until golden and vegetables are tender (approximately 35 minutes.)

Corn Free: this recipe is corn free
Soy Free: this recipe is soy free
Nut Free: prepare biscuit dough using nut-free instructions

**Serves 4**

# Chicken-n-Rice Casserole

**prep: 10 min.**
**cook: 25 min.**

## Ingredients:

4 cups chicken broth
2 cups long grain white rice

1 tablespoon oil
1 1/2 lb boneless skinless chicken (cut into 1/2" cubes)
1 1/2 cups chicken broth
1 tablespoon tapioca starch
1/4 cup cold water
1 teaspoon tarragon
1/2 teaspoon garlic powder
1/2 teaspoon salt
1/8 teaspoon ground pepper
2-3 cups frozen mixed peas and carrots.
1 cup slice mushrooms
1 1/2 cup crushed potato chips

## Method:

1. In medium pot combine broth and rice. Bring to a boil and reduce heat to low. Stir well and cover. Allow to simmer for 15 minutes. Remove from heat and keep covered to allow rice to continue to steam for an additional 5-10 minutes.
2. While rice is cooking, heat oil in large saucepan over medium heat. Add cubed chicken and cook until exterior of chicken is white. Add broth to chicken and continue to cook.
3. In small separate bowl combine tapioca starch and cold water. Mix until smooth.
4. Add tapioca mixture to chicken and broth. Mix well then add remaining ingredients except for potato chips.
5. Bring mixture to a slow boil and reduce heat to low. Simmer over low heat for 5 minutes until vegetables are tender.
6. Preheat oven to 375°F.
7. Remove from heat and mix in steamed rice. Pour into oven safe casserole dish and sprinkle top with crushed potato chips.
8. Place in oven on center rack and bake for 10 minutes or until potato chip topping is golden brown.

**Serves 4**

Corn Free: this recipe is corn free
Soy Free: this recipe is soy free
Nut Free: this recipe is nut free

# Fried Chicken Strips

**prep:** 10 min.
**cook:** 25 min.

## Ingredients:

lard or oil for frying

2 -3 lbs boneless skinless chicken (cut into 2" wide strips)
2 eggs
2/3 cup rice milk
2 1/2 cups Basic Flour Mix
3/4 cup rice flour
1 teaspoon salt
1/8 teaspoon ground pepper
1/4 teaspoon garlic powder
1/8 teaspoon paprika (optional)

## Chicken Nuggets

Cut chicken into bite sized pieces (approximately 1 1/2" x 1 1/2") and prepare using method shown above.

## Method:

*Do not prepare when children are in the immediate area due to the use of hot oil.*

1. Place lard/oil in electric fryer or cast iron dutch oven (3" deep for dutch oven) Heat oil to 375°F.
2. While oil is heating cover area with waxed paper to contain the mess.
3. In a shallow pan (pie pans work well) whisk together eggs and rice milk.
4. In another shallow pan combine flour and spices.
5. Line a plate with paper towels and set aside well away from heat source.
6. When oil has reached appropriate temperature take a piece of chicken dip it into the egg mixture then dip it into the flour mixture. Repeat for extra crispy chicken strips.
7. Place strip carefully in oil (tongs are great for this.) Repeat process until 3-4 strips are frying.
8. Cook until golden on one side then roll to cook other side until both sides are golden brown (6-9 min.) Remove strips to paper towel lined plate briefly before serving to remove any excess oil.

**Serves 4**

 **Time Saver Tip**

Double the recipe - allow cooked strips to cool on baking racks and place on cookie sheets in the freezer - when frozen transfer strips into freezer bags. To reheat place on cookie sheet in preheated 375°F oven for 7-9 minutes until hot throughout & crispy.

Corn Free: this recipe is corn free
Soy Free: this recipe is soy free
Nut Free: this recipe is nut free

# Sunday Dinner Chicken

**prep:** 10 min.
**cook:** 1 1/2 hrs

## Ingredients:

1 3-5lb whole chicken
2 teaspoons salt
1 large apple quartered (if not using rice dressing)
2 tablespoons oil
1/2 teaspoon salt
1/8 teaspoon ground pepper

Recipe for Rice Dressing (pg 96)

Recipe for Roasted Potato Medley (pg 94)

### Chicken Gravy
2 tablespoons chicken drippings
2 tablespoon tapioca flour
1 cup chicken broth
salt & pepper to taste

## Method:

1. Prepare Rice Dressing (Pg 96) if desired.
2. Preheat oven to 350°F.
3. Remove chicken from packaging. Remove Gizzard bag from cavity (may be in neck area if not in main cavity.) Rinse bird well. Pat outside dry with paper towel.
4. Loosely stuff cavity of chicken with rice dressing. If not stuffing chicken, sprinkle cavity with 2 teaspoons of salt and place quartered apple inside bird.
5. Tuck wings behind bird (similar to putting your hands behind your head.) Secure legs with poultry twine and place chicken breast side up in roasting pan.
6. Rub oil onto top and sides of chicken and sprinkle with salt and pepper.
7. Place roasting pan in center of oven and roast for 1 1/4 - 1 1/2 hours or until thickest portion of chicken registers 180°F on a meat thermometer or when meatiest portions are pierced with a fork the juices run clear rather than pink.
8. If desired, place uncooked roasted potato medley in pan with chicken 40 minutes before cooking is complete.
9. Allow chicken to sit for 5 minutes prior to carving.

### Chicken Gravy

1. Place drippings into cast iron skillet over medium heat. Add tapioca and whisk until smooth and bubbling.
2. Add chicken broth and salt & pepper. Whisking often, bring to boil and boil 1-3 min. until thick. Serve hot.

**Serves 4**

### Time Saver Tip
Make delicious chicken stock for soups by boiling the chicken carcass in 10 cups water for 1 hour. Add the end of a celery stalk, onion or fresh herbs for a savory stock. Strain and freeze for use instead of boring packaged broth.

Corn Free: this recipe is corn free
Soy Free: this recipe is soy free
Nut Free: this recipe is nut free

# Classic Chili

**prep:** 5 min.
**cook:** 25 min.

## Ingredients:

1 tablespoon oil
1 medium onion (chopped)
1 1/2 lb ground beef
2 (15oz) cans dark kidney beans (drained)
1 (28oz) can diced tomatoes (do not drain)
2 tablespoon tomato paste
3 1/2 cups water
2 teaspoons chili powder
1 teaspoon garlic powder
1 teaspoon ground cumin
2 teaspoons salt
1/4 teaspoon ground pepper

## Method:

1. Heat oil in cast iron dutch oven or heavy 5 quart pot over medium heat. Add onions and ground beef. Cook until beef is browned and onions are opaque.
2. Add remaining ingredients. Mix well.
3. Bring to slow boil then reduce heat to low and simmer for 20 minutes before serving.

Note: chili will happily simmer for 40 minutes if you have the time.

**Serve with corn bread (pg 108)**
**Serves 4**

**Time Saver Tip**

Divide leftovers into 1 1/2 cup portions and put in freezer safe containers. Freeze up to 3 months. Makes a perfect quick lunch or topping for Nachos (pg 28.)

Corn Free: this recipe is corn-free
Soy Free: this recipe is soy-free
Nut Free: this recipe is nut-free

# Taco Dinner

**prep:** 10 min.
**cook:** 10 min.

## Ingredients:

1 tablespoon oil
1 small onion (diced)
1- 11/2 lbs ground beef
2 tablespoons lemon or lime juice
2 tablespoons prepared GF/CF salsa
1/3 cup water
2 teaspoons chili powder
1/2 teaspoon garlic powder
1/2 teaspoon ground cumin
1/2 teaspoons salt or to taste
1/4 teaspoon ground pepper

### Toppings
1/4 head lettuce (shredded)
1 large tomato (diced)
GF/CF rice cheese (shredded) or Nacho
   Cheezy Sauce (pg 28)

corn taco shells or soft brown rice tortillas

## Method:

1. Heat oil in cast iron skillet over medium heat. Add onions and ground beef. Cook until beef is browned and onions are opaque.
2. Add remaining ingredients. Mix well.
3. Bring to slow boil then reduce heat to low and simmer for 3-5 minutes. Cover to keep warm before serving.

**Serve with Black Beans & Rice (pg 98)**

**Serves 4**

---

Corn Free: use the brown rice soft tortillas
Soy Free: this recipe is soy free
Nut Free: this recipe is nut free

# Beef Stew

**prep:** 10 min.
**cook:** 25 min.

## Ingredients:

- 1 1/2 lbs beef stew meat (any inexpensive cut will do) cut into 3/4"cubes
- 3 tablespoons tapioca flour
- 2 tablespoons oil
- 1 large onion (chopped into large pieces)
- 5 medium potatoes (cut into 1"cubes)
- 4 large carrots (sliced)
- 4 cups beef broth
- 2 bay leaves
- 1/2 teaspoon garlic powder
- 1/4 teaspoon rubber sage
- 1/2 teaspoon salt
- 1/8 teaspoon ground pepper

## Method:

1. Place cubed beef into zipper bag & pound to tenderize. Add tapioca flour to bag and shake well to coat evenly.
2. Heat oil in cast iron dutch oven or heavy pot over medium/ high heat. Add beef and cook until browned. Add onions and continue cooking until onions are opaque.
3. Stir in all remaining ingredients.
4. Bring to slow boil, stirring occasionally. Reduce heat to low and simmer uncovered until vegetables are tender (about 20 minutes.)

Note: stew is even better if allowed to simmer up to 45 minutes if time allows.

**Serves 4**

Corn Free: this recipe is corn-free
Soy Free: this recipe is soy free
Nut Free: this recipe is nut free

# Salisbury Steak

**prep:** 5-8 min.
**cook:** 20 min.

## Ingredients:

1 lb ground beef
1/3 cup crushed rice cereal or GF/CF breadcrumbs.
1/2 teaspoon salt
1/4 teaspoon pepper
1 egg
1 1/2 cups beef broth
1 package mushrooms (washed & sliced)
1/4 cup cold water
2 tablespoons tapioca starch

## Method:

1. In medium bowl mix ground beef, crumbs, salt pepper and egg.
2. Shape ground beef mixture into 4 oval shaped patties approximately 3/4" thick.
3. Warm cast iron skillet over medium heat 1 minute. Carefully place the 4 beef patties into skillet. Cook patties until browned, turning as needed (8 - 10 minutes.)
4. Add broth and mushrooms to skillet and bring to slow boil. Reduce heat to low. Cover and simmer 10 minutes.
5. Remove patties from skillet and place on covered dish in 200°F oven to keep warm.
6. In small bowl mix cold water and tapioca starch until dissolved. Set aside.
7. Bring broth and mushrooms to boil. Quickly stir in tapioca mixture and boil 1 minute until thick. Serve over patties.

**Serves 4**

Corn Free: this recipe is corn-free
Soy Free: this recipe is soy free
Nut Free: this recipe is nut free

# All-American Meatloaf

**prep: 10 min.**
**cook: 60-75 min.**

## Ingredients:

1 1/2 lbs ground beef
1/2 cup crushed rice cereal (or 3 slices dry GF/CF bread - grated)
2 eggs
1 cup rice milk
1 small onion (diced - about 1/4 cup)
1 tablespoon Lea & Perrins® Worcestershire sauce
1 teaspoon salt
1 teaspoon stone ground prepare mustard
1/4 teaspoon ground pepper
1/4 teaspoon rubbed sage
1/4 teaspoon garlic powder
1/2 cup GF/CF ketchup or BBQ sauce

## Method:

1. Preheat oven to 350°F.
2. In large bowl hand-mix all ingredients except GF/CF ketchup or BBQ sauce.
3. Place beef mixture into large un-greased loaf pan or casserole and shape into 3" high loaf.
4. Spoon GF/CF ketchup or BBQ sauce over top and bake uncovered for 1 to 1 1/4 hours or until cooked through.

**Serves 4**

Corn Free: use corn-free Worcestershire sauce or omit.
Soy Free: this recipe is soy free
Nut Free: this recipe is nut free

# Spaghetti & Meatballs

**prep:** 10 min.
**cook:** 30 min.

## Ingredients:

### Meatballs
1 1/2lbs ground beef
2/3 cup crushed rice cereal (or 4 slices dried GF/CF bread - grated)
1/4 cup rice milk
1 teaspoon salt
1 teaspoon Lea & Perrins® Worcestershire sauce
1/4 teaspoon ground pepper
3/4 teaspoon garlic powder (or 2 cloves crushed fresh garlic)
1/2 teaspoon oregano
1/2 teaspoon basil
1 small onion diced
2 eggs

### Sauce
2 tablespoons olive or vegetable oil
1 small onion (chopped)
1 (6oz) can tomato paste
2 cups water (an extra 1/2 cup can be added if you prefer a thinner sauce)
1 (14oz) can diced tomatoes (do not drain)
1 cup mushrooms (washed and sliced)
1 cup chopped zucchini
1/4 cup sliced black olives (optional)
1/2 teaspoon oregano
1/2 teaspoon basil
1/4 teaspoon rosemary (optional)
1/2 teaspoon salt or to taste
1/8 teaspoon ground pepper

1 package brown rice spaghetti

## Method:

### Meatballs
1. Preheat oven to 400°F.
2. In large bowl hand-mix all meatball ingredients well. Roll into 1 1/2" balls and place in 9" x 13" pan.
3. Place on center rack of oven and bake for 15 minutes turning once during cooking. (Meatballs can be cooked in large skillet over medium/high heat for 10-15 minutes if preferred.)

**While Meatballs are cooking prepare sauce.**

### Sauce
1. In large pot heat oil over medium heat. Add onions and cook until opaque.
2. Mix in all remaining sauce ingredients. Bring to slow boil and reduce heat to low and simmer.
3. Put large pot of water on stove to boil for pasta. When water begins to boil, cook pasta according to package instructions.
4. When meatballs have cooked for the allotted period, carefully remove them from pan and place in sauce. Allow meatballs/sauce to simmer over very low heat until pasta is ready. (You may want to cover pot loosely to prevent spattering)
5. Drain pasta and top with meatballs and sauce.

**Serves 4**

---

Corn Free: use corn-free Worcestershire sauce or omit.
Soy Free: this recipe is soy free
Nut Free: this recipe is nut free

# Ham & Potato Casserole

**prep:** 5 min.
**cook:** 25 min.

## Ingredients:

6-7 medium potatoes
1/4 cup cold water
1 1/2 tablespoons tapioca starch
1 tablespoon bacon grease (or oil)
1 cup cubed ham
1 1/2 cups chicken broth or ham stock
1 cup sliced mushrooms
1 cup frozen peas
1/2 teaspoon salt
1/8 teaspoon ground pepper
1/4 teaspoon garlic powder
1/4 teaspoon chives (optional)

1 1/2 cups crushed potato chips

## Method:

1. Wash & poke 2 holes in each of the potatoes. Place on microwave safe plate and microwave on high for 10 minutes. While potatoes are cooking prepare sauce.
2. Preheat oven to 375°F.
3. In small bowl combine cold water and tapioca starch. Mix until smooth then set aside.
4. Heat bacon grease in cast iron skillet over medium flame. Add ham and cook until golden.
5. Add broth, vegetables and spices. Bring mixture to a boil. Stirring contantly, add tapioca mixture. Return sauce to boil and allow to boil for 1-2 minutes until sauce begins to thicken. Remove from heat and cover to keep warm.
6. Remove potatoes from microwave - using oven mitt or fork to hold hot potatoes, slice cooked potatoes carefully and place in large bowl.
7. Pour sauce over sliced potatoes and mix carefully. Pour into oven safe casserole and sprinkle with crushed potato chips.
8. Place on center rack of oven and bake until golden (10-15 minutes.)

**Serves 4**

Corn Free: ensure ham used is not "glazed" with corn syrup
Soy Free: this recipe is soy free
Nut Free: this recipe is nut free

# Pizza

prep: 25 min.
cook: 30 min.

## Ingredients:

### Crusts

**Dry**
1 3/4 cup rice flour
1 1/4 cups tapioca starch
1 1/2 teaspoon xantham gum
1 packet unflavored gelatin
1 tablespoon egg replacer
2 tablespoons sugar
1/3 cup almond meal
1 teaspoon salt
2 1/2 teaspoons yeast

**Wet**
4 egg whites (can use reconstituted powdered egg whites)
3 tablespoons oil
1 teaspoon vinegar
1 1/2 cups + 2 tablespoons warm water

### Sauce
1 (6oz) can tomato paste
1 1/2 cups water
1/2 teaspoon garlic powder
1/2 teaspoon salt
1/2 teaspoon italian seasonings (oregano/basil)
1/8 teaspoon ground pepper

### Toppings
Mozzarella style casein free rice or soy cheese
pepperoni or meats of your choice
vegetables of your choice (sliced)

## Method:

1. Preheat oven to 400°F.
2. Place parchment paper on 2 pizza pans.
3. In medium bowl mix dry ingredients.
4. In large bowl blend together wet ingredients.
5. Add dry ingredients to wet and mix until incorporated. Using an electric mixer blend on high for 3 minutes until smooth.
6. Divide dough evenly on parchment covered pans. Using a rubber spatula sprayed with oil, spread dough from center towards edges until desired thickness. Let rest/rise in warm draft free area for 10-15 minutes then prick crusts with a fork in several places.
7. Place crusts in center racks of ovens and bake for 10-12 minutes.
8. While crusts are baking, whisk all sauce ingredients together in a medium bowl and set aside.
9. Remove crusts from oven. Spread sauce over crusts, sprinkle with cheese and toppings.
10. Bake for 15-20 minutes until golden brown & bubbly.

**Makes 2 Pizzas**

 **Time Saver Tip**
Instead of 2 large pizzas - divide dough into 12 individual sized crusts. Bake for 8-10 minutes. Cool on wire racks. Cover with toppings of your choice and freeze for perfect frozen individual pizzas. Bake in preheated 400°F oven until golden and bubbly.

Corn Free: this recipe is corn free
Soy Free: use casein free rice cheese.
Nut Free: replace almond meal with 1/8 cup sorghum flour

# Side Dishes

## French Fries

*Do not prepare these recipes when children are in the immediate area due to the use of hot oil.*

**prep:** 5 min.
**cook:** 5-7 min.

### Ingredients:

lard or oil for frying

2 lbs potatoes or sweet potatoes (4 large)
salt

### Method:

1. Wash and dry potatoes. Cut into 1/4 - 3/8" wide long strips. Chill sliced potatoes in refrigerator in bowl covered with plastic wrap.
2. Place lard in electric fryer or cast iron dutch oven (3" deep for dutch oven) & heat to 375-378°F.
3. Fill basket 1/4 full with sliced potatoes (if using basket) or gently place approximately 1/4 - 1/2 lb of potatoes into oil (use a long handled fork to keep potatoes separated and fry until golden (5-7 minutes.)
4. Drain fries on folded paper bag or plate draped with paper towels well away from heat source.

## Onion Rings

**prep:** 10 min.
**cook:** 5-7 min.

### Ingredients:

lard or oil for frying
1 large onion (sliced into 1/2-1" thick slices)

**Dry**
2/3 cup Flour Mix
1/3 cup rice flour
1 teaspoon baking powder
1 teaspoon salt (or seasoning salt)
1 cup crushed Rice Chex®

**Wet**
1 egg
1 cup rice milk

Corn Free: this recipe is corn free
Soy Free: this recipe is soy free
Nut Free: this recipe is nut free

### Method:

1. Place lard in electric fryer or cast iron dutch oven (3" deep for dutch oven) & heat to 375°F
2. Separate onion slices into rings and set aside.
3. Combine dry ingredients in shallow pan. Set aside.
4. Whisk together wet ingredients.
5. Dip onion ring into egg mixture to coat evenly then dip onion ring into flour mixture (repeat for extra crispy rings.)
6. Carefully place (3-4 rings/batch) in oil and fry until golden. Drain onion rings on folded paper bag or plate draped with paper towels well away from heat source.

**Serves 4**

## Green Beans Almondine

**prep:** 5 min.
**Cook:** 5 min.

### Ingredients:

1 tablespoon oil
14 oz frozen or fresh whole green beans
1/3 cup sliced almonds
dash garlic powder
dash salt
dash ground or cracked pepper

### Method:

1. Heat oil in cast iron skillet over medium/high flame.
2. Being careful to avoid spattering oil, add remaining ingredients. Stir while cooking until beans are dark green and tender (3-4 minutes.)
3. Serve immediately.

**Serves 4**

## Glazed Carrots

**prep:** 5 min.
**Cook:** 15 min.

### Ingredients:

1 1/2 lbs carrots
water for steaming (approximately 1 cup)
1 cup water
1/3 cup packed brown sugar
1/2 teaspoon salt
1/2 teaspoon grated orange peel
2 teaspoons oil

### Method:

1. Peel and cut carrots. Place in saucepan in steamer basket or alone and add 1 cup water for steaming. Cover and cook over medium/high heat until carrots are tender.
2. While carrots are steaming, combine remaining ingredients in medium saucepan over medium heat. Cook until bubbly then remove from heat & cover.
3. When carrots are tender place in sauce and cook over medium heat until glazed (3-5 minutes.)

**Serves 4**

Corn Free: these recipes are corn free
Soy Free: these recipes are soy free
Nut Free: omit almonds

# Roasted Potato Medley

**prep: 5 min.**
**cook: 30-40 min.**

## Ingredients:

4 medium russet potatoes
4 medium sweet potatoes
3 tablespoons oil
1/2 teaspoon garlic powder
1/2 teaspoon thyme
1/4 teaspoon rosemary (optional)
1/8 teaspoon ground pepper
1/2 teaspoon salt

## Method:

1. Preheat oven to 400°F.
2. Wash and cut potatoes into 1 1/2" cubes. Place potatoes into gallon zipper bag.
3. Place remaining ingredients into gallon zipper bag. Seal bag and shake until potatoes are evenly covered.
4. Place potatoes into shallow pan and bake, turning as needed until fork tender and golden (approximately 25-35 minutes.)

**Serves 4**

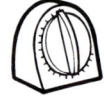

### Time Saver Tip

Potatoes can be placed in roasting pan with Sunday Dinner Chicken (pg 72) for the final 40 minutes of roasting.

Corn Free: this recipe is corn free
Soy Free: this recipe is soy free
Nut Free: this recipe is nut free

# Classic Rice Dressing

**prep: 10 min.**
**cook: 20 min.**

## Ingredients:

3 1/2 cups broth/stock (chicken or beef depending on what you are serving it with)
1 1/2 cups long grain white rice
1/2 cup wild rice (optional - if not using decrease broth to 3 1/8 cups
2 tablespoons oil
1 small onion diced
4 stalks celery chopped
1 medium apple (peeled and chopped)
1 cup mushrooms (sliced)
1/2 cup raisins
1/2 cup broth/stock

## Method:

1. Place rice and broth into large saucepan. Bring to boil over medium/high flame. When broth reaches a boil reduce heat to low, stir once and cover. Allow to simmer for 20 minutes.
2. While rice cooks, heat oil in a cast iron skillet over medium flame. Add onion and celery and cook stirring often until onions are opaque.
3. Add remaining ingredients and bring to boil. Cook 1 minute and remove from heat. Cover to keep warm.
4. When rice is done steaming add vegetables and stir gently to blend.

**Serves 4**

Corn Free: this recipe is corn free
Soy Free: this recipe is soy free
Nut Free: this recipe is nut free

# Black Beans & Rice

**prep: 5 min.**
**cook: 20 min.**

## Ingredients:

1 tablespoon oil
1 small onion diced
2 cups water
1 (15oz) can black beans (drained)
1 (15oz) can diced tomatoes (drain approximately half of the juice)
1/2 teaspoon ground cumin
1 teaspoon chili powder
1 teaspoon salt
1/8 teaspoon ground pepper
1 cup long grain white rice

## Method:

1. Heat oil in medium saucepan over medium flame. Add onion and cook stirring often until opaque.
2. Add remaining ingredients, stir well and bring to boil. Reduce heat to low, stir once and cover. Allow to simmer for 20 minutes or until rice is tender.
3. Remove from heat and keep covered until ready to serve. Toss gently with fork before serving.

**Serves 4**

Corn Free: this recipe is corn free
Soy Free: this recipe is soy free
Nut Free: this recipe is nut free

## Maple Butternut Squash

**prep:** 5 min.
**cook:** 40 min.

### Ingredients:

1 medium sized butternut squash
4 tablespoons pure maple syrup
1/4 teaspoon salt
1/4 teaspoon ground pepper

 **Time Saver Tip**
Squash can be cooked on high in the microwave, loosely covered, for 8-10 minutes until tender throughout.

### Method:

1. Preheat oven to 350°F.
2. Wash squash well and cut in half the long way. Scoop out and discard the seeds.
3. Place squash in large glass baking dish skin-side-down. Drizzle lightly with maple syrup and sprinkle with salt and pepper.
4. Bake uncovered 40 minutes or until tender.

**Serves 4**

## Mixed Veggies with Cheezy Sauce

**prep:** 5 min.
**cook:** 7 min.

### Ingredients:

12oz package frozen vegetables
1/2 - 1 cup water (for steaming)
1 1/2 tablespoons oil
2 tablespoons tapioca
1 tablespoon rice flour
1 1/2 cups rice milk
4 tablespoons nutritional yeast
1 teaspoon salt
1 tablespoon lemon juice
1 tablespoon sesame tahini
1/4 teaspoon finely ground paprika

### Method:

1. Place water in medium saucepan. Add vegetables (preferably in a steamer basket) and cover. Cook on medium high heat until vegetables are tender (5-7 minutes.)
2. In small saucepan heat oil over low flame and whisk in flours. Stir until bubbly and flour begins to turn golden (2-3 minutes.)
3. Whisk in remaining ingredients and bring to a boil. Cook 3 minutes or until thick.
4. Remove from heat and cover to keep warm - serve on top of freshly steamed vegetables.

**Serves 4**

Corn Free: these recipes are corn free
Soy Free: these recipes are soy free
Nut Free: these recipes are nut free

# Breads

# White Sandwich Bread

prep: 8 min.
rise: 30-60 min
bake: 50-55 min.

## Ingredients:

### Dry
1 cup rice flour
1 cup tapioca starch
1 cup arrowroot starch
2 1/4 teaspoons xantham gum
1 1/2 teaspoon unflavored gelatin
1 1/2 teaspoon egg replacer
1 teaspoon salt
3 tablespoons sugar
1/3 cup almond meal
2 1/4 teaspoons yeast

### Wet
1 egg (room temperature)
2 egg whites (room temperature - reconstituted powdered egg whites can be used)
1/4 cup softened coconut oil (**not** extra-virgin)
3/4 teaspoon vinegar
1 tablespoon honey
1 1/2 cups warm water

## Method:

1. Grease and lightly flour (rice flour) 2 medium (4.5" x 8") glass bread pans.
2. In medium bowl combine all dry ingredients.
3. In large bowl use electric mixer to beat all wet ingredients except water. When well blended add water and mix carefully.
4. Mix dry ingredients into wet. When well incorporated scrape sides and beat with electric mixer on high for 3-4 minutes.
5. Pour into prepared pans. Cover with plastic wrap and then drape with a dishtowel and set in a warm, draft-free area to rise.
6. Preheat oven to 375°F.
7. Allow to rise until double (30-40 min. if using quick rise yeast, 50-60 min. for regular yeast.)
   **Note: do not** allow dough to rise over top edge of pan before baking - it may sink after it cools. It tastes fine, but isn't as pretty a loaf.
8. Place in center rack of oven. Bake for 10 minutes. Drape loosely with tin foil to prevent over-browning and bake an additional 35-40 minutes until bread sounds hollow when tapped on top.
9. Allow to cool completely in pan before slicing.

## Rolls

Cover baking sheet with parchment paper and drop 1/2 cup scoops of dough onto pan. Cover loosely with plastic wrap and let rise 30-30 minutes. Bake on center rack of 375°F oven for 20-25 minutes or until golden and rolls sound hollow when tapped.

Corn Free: this recipe is corn free
Soy Free: this recipe is soy free
Nut Free: replace almond meal with 1/8 cup potato starch - the texture is not quite as nice but bread is still soft and flavorful.

# Golden Cornbread

**prep:** 5 min.
**bake:** 18-25 min.

## Ingredients:

1 1/2 cups yellow cornmeal
1/2 cup Basic Flour Mix
3/4 teaspoon xantham gum
2 teaspoons baking powder
1 teaspoon sugar
1 teaspoon salt
1/2 teaspoon baking soda
1/4 cup oil
1 1/2 cups rice milk
1 teaspoon vinegar
2 eggs

## Method:

1. Preheat oven to 450°F.
2. Oil cast iron skillet or grease 8" x 8" baking pan.
3. In medium bowl mix all dry ingredients and then add remaining ingredients and blend until well incorporated.
4. Pour into pan and bake for 18-25 minutes or until wooden toothpick inserted into center comes out clean.

# Biscuits

**prep:** 5 min.
**Cook:** 12 min.

## Ingredients:

2 egg whites

**Dry**
1 2/3 cups Basic Flour Mix
1/3 cup almond meal
1/4 cup rice flour
1 1/2 teaspoons xantham gum
1 1/2 teaspoons baking powder
1 teaspoon baking soda
1/2 teaspoon salt
1 1/2 teaspoons egg replacer

**Wet**
3/4 cup rice milk
1 teaspoon vinegar
2 tablespoons oil

spray oil

## Method:

1. Preheat oven to 475°F.
2. Cover baking sheet with parchment paper
3. In separate bowl beat egg whites until stiff & glossy. set aside.
4. In medium sized bowl combine all dry ingredients.
5. In small bowl mix wet ingredients.
6. Add wet ingredients and egg whites to dry and gently mix until incorporated.
7. Dust hands with tapioca starch and gently form dough into 2 1/2" wide x 1" thick biscuits.
8. Place biscuits on prepared baking sheet and spray tops lightly with oil.
9. Bake on center rack until golden (8-12 min.)

Corn Free: Golden cornbread: N/A  Biscuits: use corn free baking powder
Soy Free: these recipes are soy free
Nut Free: Golden cornbread: recipe is nut free  Biscuits: replace almond meal with 2 tablespoons sorghum flour

# Banana Nut Bread

prep: 5 min.
bake: 45-50 min.

## Ingredients:

### Wet
1 cup sugar
1/8 cup oil
1/8 cup applesauce
2 eggs (room temperature)
1 1/2 cups mashed ripe bananas (3-4 medium)
1/4 cup water

### Dry
1 2/3 cups Basic Flour Mix
1 1/2 teaspoons xantham gum
1 1/2 teaspoons baking soda
1 1/2 teaspoons egg replacer
1/2 teaspoon salt
1/2 teaspoon baking powder

1/2 cup chopped nuts (optional)

### Topping (optional)
1 1/2 tablespoons sugar
1/2 teaspoon cinnamon

## Method:

1. Grease 2 medium (4.5" x 8.5") glass bread pans or one extra-large pan.
2. Preheat oven to 350°F F.
3. In large bowl use electric mixer to combine wet ingredients.
4. In small bowl combine dry ingredients.
5. Add dry ingredients to wet and mix with electric mixer on medium until well incorporated.
6. Stir in nuts and pour into prepared pans.
7. In small bowl or shaker mix sugar and cinnamon and sprinkle lightly over batter.
8. Place on center rack of oven and bake 45-50 minutes for 2 loaves and 50-60 minutes for extra large loaf or until wooden toothpick inserted in center comes out clean.

*If baking one extra large loaf - you may wish to drape with tin foil halfway through baking to prevent over-browning of top.

Note: loaves will settle as they cool to create a moist, soft bread.

**Time Saver Tip**
As bananas get too ripe to eat - peel and place in quart sized freezer bags and freeze until ready to bake banana bread. Thaw until easily mashed and use as you would fresh bananas.

Corn Free: use corn-free baking powder
Soy Free: this recipe is soy free
Nut Free: omit chopped nuts

# Dessert

# Pineapple Upside-Down Cake

**prep:** 10 min.
**bake:** 20-30 min.

## Ingredients:

2 tablespoons melted coconut oil
1/3 cup packed brown sugar
1 (8.25oz) can of sliced pineapple
6-9 dried or fresh cherries (**do not** use artificially colored maraschino cherries)

### Dry
1 1/2 cups + 1/8 cup Basic Flour Mix
1 teaspoons baking powder
1 teaspoons egg replacer
1 teaspoon xantham gum
1/2 teaspoon salt

### Wet
1/2 cup shortening
3/4 cup sugar
2 eggs (room temperature)
1 teaspoons GF/CF vanilla
3/4 cup cream soda

## Method:

1. Grease 9" round pan.
2. Preheat oven to 350°F.
3. In small bowl combine melted coconut oil and brown sugar. Sprinkle into bottom of prepared pan. Arrange sliced pineapple and place cherries in center of rings. Set aside.
4. In medium bowl mix dry ingredients and set aside.
5. In large bowl, use electric mixer to cream together shortening and sugar.
6. Add eggs one at a time, beating until smooth then beat in vanilla.
7. To shortening mixture add dry ingredients and cream soda. Mix until just blended and pour batter over pineapple slices.
8. Bake for 20-30 minutes or until wooden toothpick inserted into center of cake comes out clean.
9. Remove from oven. Let sit 2 minutes then place cake plate upside-down on top of pan. Using oven mitts to hold both pan and plate - quickly and carefully invert.

Serve warm with piña colada ice cream

**Serves 4-6**

Corn Free: use corn-free baking powder & cream soda made with cane sugar
Soy Free: this recipe is soy free
Nut Free: this recipe is nut free

# Classic Vanilla Layer Cake

prep: 10 min.
bake: 20-45 min.

## Ingredients:

**Dry**
3 1/4 cups Basic Flour Mix
2 teaspoons baking powder
2 teaspoons egg replacer
1 teaspoon salt
1 1/2 teaspoon xantham gum

**Wet**
1 cup shortening
1 1/2 cup sugar
4 eggs (room temperature)
2 teaspoons GF/CF vanilla
1 1/2 cups cream soda

**Chocolate Frosting**
2/3 cup shortening
2/3 cup cocoa powder
4 cups powdered confectioners sugar
1 tablespoon GF/CF vanilla
4-6 tablespoons rice milk

## Method:

1. Grease 3 round 8" pans (for perfect layers cut a circle of parchment paper to fit the bottom of each round pan) or a 9"x13" pan.
2. Preheat oven to 350°F.
3. In medium bowl mix dry ingredients and set aside.
4. In large bowl, use electric mixer to cream together shortening and sugar.
5. Add eggs one at a time, beating until smooth then beat in vanilla.
6. To shortening mixture, add dry ingredients and cream soda. Mix until just blended and divide batter amongst the pans.
7. Bake 8" rounds for 20-25 minutes and 9"x13" pan for 35-45 minutes or until wooden toothpick inserted into center of cake comes out clean. Cool completely before frosting.

### Chocolate Frosting

1. Cream shortening with electric mixer until fluffy & smooth.
2. Add remaining ingredients and beat until spreading consistency.
3. Frost cooled cakes as desired.

**Hint:** for easier frosting of cake, dip knife into very hot water each time you use it. This prevents the frosting from sticking to knife rather than the cake.

**Serves 6-8**

Corn Free: use corn-free baking powder & powdered sugar (an electric coffee grinder can make powdered sugar in a pinch - add 1/4 teaspoon tapioca starch per cup. Use cream soda made with cane sugar.
Soy Free: this recipe is soy free
Nut Free: this recipe is nut free

# All-American Chocolate Chip Cookies

**prep:** 10 min.
**bake:** 8-10 min.

## Ingredients:

### Wet
3/4 cup sugar
3/4 cup brown sugar
1/4 cup shortening
1/2 cup lard
1 egg (room temperature)
1 teaspoon GF/CF vanilla
1 tablespoon honey

### Dry
2 3/4 cups Basic Flour Mix
1 teaspoon baking soda
1/2 teaspoon salt
1 1/2 teaspoons xantham gum

1 cup GF/CF semi-sweet chocolate chips

## Method:

1. Line baking sheets with parchment paper.
2. Preheat oven to 350°F.
3. Using electric mixer cream together sugar, shortening and lard until smooth & fluffy. Add remaining wet ingredients and set aside.
4. In medium bowl combine all dry ingredients.
5. Add dry ingredients to wet and mix well.
6. Add semi-sweet chocolate chips and stir until well incorporated.
7. Place heaping teaspoons of dough onto prepared pans approximately 1 1/2" apart.
8. Place pans on center rack of preheated oven and bake until light brown. (8-10 minutes.)

**Makes 4 dozen**
**Store in airtight container in cool dry place**

### Time Saver Tip
Double recipe and divide dough in half. Roll half of dough into cylinder shape and wrap in plastic wrap. Place in freezer bag and freeze. To bake simply thaw dough in refrigerator and follow steps #7 - 8.

Corn Free: this recipe is corn free
Soy Free: ensure that GF/CF chocolate chips used are soy free
Nut Free: this recipe is nut free

# Snickerdoodles

prep: 10 min.
chill: 20 min.
bake: 8-12 min.

## Ingredients:

**Wet**
1 1/2 cups sugar
1/2 cup shortening
1/4 cup coconut oil
2 teaspoons GF/CF vanilla
2 eggs (room temperature)
1 teaspoon honey

**Dry**
3 1/8 cups Basic Flour Mix
2 teaspoons cream of tartar
1 1/4 teaspoons baking soda
3/4 teaspoon salt
2 teaspoons xantham gum

**Cinnamon Sugar**
2 tablespoons sugar
1 teaspoon cinnamon

## Method:

1. With electric mixer cream together shortening, sugar and coconut oil. Beat in remaining wet ingredients and set aside.
2. In medium bowl mix dry ingredients.
3. Add dry to wet and blend well.
4. Chill dough in refrigerator for 20 minutes. (or freezer for 10 minutes.)
5. In small bowl combine sugar and cinnamon and set aside.
6. Preheat oven to 375°F.
7. Line baking sheets with parchment paper.
8. Remove dough from refrigerator. Using melon-baller or teaspoon, scoop out dough and form into 1" balls. Roll balls in cinnamon sugar, place on pan and press gently with heel of hand to flatten slightly.
9. Bake in center rack of oven for 8-12 minutes until light golden.

**Makes 4 dozen cookies**
**Store in airtight container in cool, dry place**

**Time Saver Tip**
Double recipe and divide dough in half. Roll half of dough into cylinder shape and wrap in plastic wrap. Place in freezer bag and freeze. To bake simply thaw dough in refrigerator and follow steps 5-10.

Corn Free: this recipe is corn free
Soy Free: this recipe is soy free
Nut Free: this recipe is nut free

# Decadent Fudge Brownies

**prep:** 5 min.
**bake:** 23-30 min.

## Ingredients:

### Wet
1 cup sugar
1/2 cup coconut oil (**not** extra-virgin)
1 teaspoon vanilla
2 eggs (room temperature)
1 tablespoon honey

### Dry
2/3 cup Basic Flour Mix
3/4 teaspoon xantham gum
1/2 cup cocoa powder
1/2 teaspoon baking powder
1/2 teaspoon salt
1/2 cup nuts (optional)
1/2 cup GF/CF semi-sweet chocolate chips (optional)

## Method:

1. Grease *or* line 8"x8" pan with parchment paper (paper keeps edges tender and you can lift out brownies for easy cutting.)
2. Preheat oven to 350°F.
3. With electric mixer cream together wet ingredients.
4. In medium bowl blend all dry ingredients except nuts and chips.
5. Add dry ingredients to wet and mix until incorporated. Add nuts and chips and mix evenly.
6. Spread batter in pan and bake on center rack of oven for 23-30 minutes or until wooden toothpick inserted in center comes out clean.

**Makes a dozen brownies**

Corn Free: use corn free baking powder
Soy Free: use soy free GF/CF Chocolate chips or omit (these hold their own even without the chips)
Nut Free: exclude nuts - shortening can be used in place of coconut oil if sensitive.

# Peanut Butter Cookies

prep: 5 min.
bake: 7-9 min.

## Ingredients:

**Wet**
3/4 cup peanut butter
1/3 cup + 1 tablespoon shortening
1/2 cup brown sugar
1/2 cup sugar
1 egg (room temperature)
1 tablespoon honey (omit if you prefer a crispier cookie)

**Dry**
1 3/4 cups + 1 tablespoon Basic Flour Mix
1 teaspoon xantham gum
1 teaspoon soda
3/4 teaspoon salt

## Method:

1. Preheat oven to 350°F.
2. Line baking sheets with parchment paper.
3. With electric mixer cream together wet ingredients and set aside.
4. In medium bowl mix dry ingredients.
5. Add dry to wet and blend well with electric mixer.
6. Chill dough in refrigerator for 15 minutes if time permits (optional)
7. Using melon baller or teaspoon, scoop out dough and form into 1" balls. Place on pan and press gently with tines of fork, turn fork and repeat to crisscross.
8. Bake in center rack of preheated oven for 7-9 minutes until light golden.

**Makes 4 dozen cookies**
**Store in airtight container in cool, dry place**

**Time Saver Tip**
Double recipe and divide dough in half. Roll half of dough into cylinder shape and wrap in plastic wrap. Place in freezer bag and freeze. To bake simply thaw dough in refrigerator and follow steps 7-9.

Corn Free: this recipe is corn free
Soy Free: this recipe is soy free
Nut Free: try using Sunbutter® in place of peanut butter

# Dessert Pizza

prep: 20 min.
bake: 30-40 min.

## Ingredients:

Prepared pizza crust (pg 88) on parchment covered pan

1/2 - 1 cup prepared apple compote (pg 32), GF/CF Pie filling or fruit preserves.

### Crumb topping
1/2 cup tapioca starch
1/4 cup rice flour
1/2 cup packed brown sugar
1/3 cup almond meal
1/2 teaspoon cinnamon
1/4 cup shortening
1 teaspoon GF/CF vanilla

### Glaze
1 cup powdered sugar
1 1/2 tablespoons rice milk
1 teaspoon GF/CF vanilla

## Method:

1. Preheat oven to 400°F.
2. Allow crust to rise/rest in warm place for 15 minutes.
3. Bake crust on center rack of oven for 10 minutes.
4. While crust bakes combine all ingredients for crumb topping and cut together (mix) with pastry cutter or two butter knives until well incorporated.
5. Remove crust from oven and spread fruit evenly over top.
6. Sprinkle with crumb topping and bake on center rack of oven for 20-30 minutes or until bottom of crust is golden (peek by carefully lifting an edge up with a spatula or fork.
7. During the last few minutes of baking combine glaze ingredients in a small bowl and mix well.
8. Remove from oven and allow to cool for 3-5 minutes. Drizzle with glaze and serve warm.

Corn Free: use corn free powdered sugar or omit glaze
Soy Free: this recipe is soy free
Nut Free: replace almond meal with 1/8 cup sorghum flour & use pizza crust made with nut free instructions

# Cherry Cobbler

**prep:** 10 min.
**bake:** 25-35 min.

## Ingredients:

3 tablespoons tapioca starch
1 cup sugar
1 teaspoon lemon juice
5 cups pitted sour cherries (fresh, frozen or 2 (16oz) cans - drained)
2 teaspoons GF/CF almond extract (optional)

### Dry
1 cup rice flour
3/4 cup tapioca starch
1/4 cup almond meal
1 1/2 teaspoons xantham gum
2/3 cup sugar
2 teaspoons baking powder
1 teaspoon baking soda
1/2 teaspoon salt

### Wet
2 teaspoons GF/CF vanilla
1/3 cup oil
2 eggs (room temperature)
3/4 cup rice milk

## Method:

1. Preheat oven to 375°F.
2. Grease small rectangular cake pan (approximately 7.5" x 11.5") and set aside.
3. In medium saucepan mix tapioca starch and sugar. Add lemon juice and cherries. Cook over medium flame, stirring constantly.
4. When cherries begin to boil reduce heat to low and continue to stir while cherries simmer (2-3 minutes until sauce thickens.) Remove from heat and cover to keep warm.
5. In medium mixing bowl combine all dry ingredients.
6. In small mixing bowl whisk together all wet ingredients.
7. Add wet ingredients to dry and mix.
8. Pour batter into prepared pan.
9. Pour/spread cherries evenly over batter.
10. Place on center rack of oven and bake for 25-35 minutes or until wooden toothpick inserted into center (of batter portion) comes out clean.

**Serves 6-8**

Corn Free: use corn free baking powder
Soy Free: this recipe is soy free
Nut Free: replace almond meal with 1/8 cup sorghum flour

## Banana Split Ice Cream

prep: 10 min.
process: 40 min.
freeze: 4-8 hrs

### Ingredients:

- 2 (14oz) cans of coconut milk
- 1/2 teaspoon salt
- 1/2 cup + 2 tablespoons sugar
- 1 cup strawberries (sliced)
- 1 heaping tablespoon powdered egg whites
- 1/2 banana
- 1/2 cup strawberries (diced)

### Method:

1. In medium saucepan combine 1 cup coconut milk, sugar and salt. Heat over low flame, stirring often until sugar is completely dissolved. Remove from heat.
2. Stir in remaining coconut milk and cool to room temperature (can be refrigerated to speed up process.)
3. When cool pour into blender. Add powdered egg whites and blend on high for 3-4 minutes. Add cup *sliced* strawberries and blend for 30 seconds to mix.
4. Dice up banana and add both banana and *diced* strawberries to mixture.
5. Place mixture into ice cream maker and process according to manufacturer's instructions.
6. Spoon mixture into 1.5 quart sized freezer safe container and freeze until firm or overnight.

## Piña Colada Ice Cream

### Ingredients:

- 2 (14oz) cans of coconut milk
- 1/2 cup + 2 tablespoons sugar
- 1/2 teaspoon salt
- 1 teaspoons GF/CF vanilla
- 1 heaping tablespoon powdered egg whites
- 1 cup crushed pineapple (drained)

### Method:

1. In medium saucepan combine 1 cup coconut milk, sugar and salt. Heat over low flame, stirring often until sugar is completely dissolved. Remove from heat.
2. Stir in remaining coconut milk and cool to room temperature (can be refrigerated to speed up process.)
3. When cool pour into blender. Add powdered egg whites and vanilla and blend on high for 3-4 minutes.
4. Add pineapple and place mixture into ice cream maker. Process according to manufacturer's instructions.
5. Spoon mixture into 1.5 quart sized freezer safe container and freeze until firm or overnight.

**Makes approximately 1.25 Qt of each**

Corn Free: this recipe is corn free
Soy Free: this recipe is soy free
Nut Free: this recipe is nut free

## Hot Fudge Sauce

**prep: 2 min.**
**cook: 6 min.**

### Ingredients:

1/4 cup cocoa powder
1 tablespoon tapioca starch
1/2 cup sugar
1/4 teaspoon salt
1 1/2 cups rice milk
1/2 teaspoon GF/CF vanilla

### Method:

1. In small saucepan mix cocoa, tapioca starch, sugar and salt until well incorporated.
2. Add 3/4 cup rice milk and mix well. Cook, stirring constantly over low flame until; smooth and bubbles form on edges.
3. Stir in remaining 3/4 cup rice milk.
4. Stirring constantly bring sauce to a boil and cook for 3-4 minutes.
5. Remove from heat and stir in vanilla.
6. Let sauce cool slightly and pour into glass jar with lid.

**Make about 1 3/4 cups**

**Perfect topping for ice-cream and fruit, it also makes great chocolate rice milk !**

## Fruit Smoothies

**prep: 3 min.**
**blend 3-4 min.**

### Ingredients:

1 cup juice or rice milk
2 cups ice
1 cup strawberries, peaches or other soft seasonal fruit
1 ripe banana
2 tablespoons honey (or to taste)

### Method:

1. Pour ice and juice into blender and process until ice is well crushed.
2. Add remaining ingredients and blend until smooth.
3. Serve immediately.

**Serves 2**

Corn Free: these recipes are corn free
Soy Free: these recipes are soy free
Nut Free: these recipes are nut free

# Index

# Index

All-American Chocolate Chip Cookies, 118
Apple compote, 32
Banana Nut Bread, 110
Banana Split Ice Cream, 130
Basic Mayonnaise, 19

Basic Flour Mix, 14
BBQ Sauce, 20
Beef
    Beef Stew, 78
    Chili, 74
    Meatloaf, 82
    Salisbury Steak, 80
    Sloppy Joes, 54
    Spaghetti & Meatballs, 84
    Taco Dinner, 76
Beef Stew, 78
Biscuits & gravy, 42
Biscuits, 108
Black Beans & Rice, 98
Bread
    Banana Nut Bread, 110
    Biscuits, 108
    Golden Cornbread, 108
    Rolls, 106
    White Sandwich Bread, 106
Breakfast scramble, 40
Cakes
    Classic Vanilla Layer Cake, 116
    Pineapple Upside-Down Cake, 114
Casseroles
    Chicken–n-Rice Casserole, 68
    Ham & Potato Casserole, 86
Cherry Cobbler, 128
Chicken
    Chicken Noodle soup, 46
    Chicken Nuggets, 70
    Chicken Pot Pie, 66
    Chicken Salad, 58
    Chicken–n Rice Casserole, 68
    Fried Chicken Strips, 70
    Quick-n-Easy Pan Seared Chicken , 60
    Sunday Dinner Chicken, 72
Chili, 74
Classic American Ketchup, 19
Classic Snack Mix, 22
Classic Tomato Soup, 48
Classic Vanilla Layer Cake, 116
Condiments
    Basic Mayonnaise, 19
    Classic American Ketchup, 19
    Thousand Island Dressing, 20
    BBQ Sauce, 20
Cookies
    All-American Chocolate Chip Cookies, 118
    Peanut Butter Cookies, 124
    Snickerdoodles, 120
Corn-free
    Corn-free Syrup, 18
    Corn-free Baking Powder, 18
    Basic Mayonnaise, 19
    Classic American Ketchup, 19
    Thousand Island Dressing, 20
    BBQ Sauce, 20
Corn-free Baking Powder, 18
Corn-free Syrup, 18
Corn Dogs, 56
Decadent Fudge Brownies, 122
Dessert Pizza, 126
Eggs
    Breakfast scramble, 40
    Oven Omelet, 38
Flours, 14
Franks & Beans, 52
French Fries, 92

# Index

French toast, 36
Fried Chicken Strips, 70
Fruit Smoothies, 132
Gelatin Blocks, 24
Glazed Carrots, 102
Golden Cornbread, 108
Green Beans Almondine, 102
Grilled Cheezy Sandwiches, 48
Ham & Potato Casserole, 86
Hash browns, 40
Hot Fudge Sauce, 132
Ice cream
- Banana Split Ice Cream, 130
- Piña Colada Ice Cream, 130

Italian Parmesan Seasonings, 26
Juice Gelatin, 24
Mac-n–Cheez, 62
Maple Butternut Squash, 100
Meatloaf, 82
Mixed Veggies with Cheezy Sauce, 100
Nachos, 28
Onion Rings, 92
Oven Omelet, 38
Pancakes, 32
Peanut Butter Cookies, 124
Piña Colada Ice Cream, 130
Pineapple Upside-Down Cake, 114
Pizza, 88
Potatoes
- French Fries, 92
- Ham & Potato Casserole, 86
- Hash browns, 40
- Roasted Potato Medley, 94

Quick-n-Easy Pan Seared Chicken , 60
Rice Dressing, 96
Roasted Potato Medley, 94
Rolls, 106
Salisbury Steak, 80
Sloppy Joes, 54

Snacks
- Traditional Popcorn, 26
- Sweet-n-Spicy Snack Mix, 22
- Classic Snack Mix, 22
- Nachos, 28
- Gelatin Blocks, 24
- Juice Gelatin, 24

Snickerdoodles, 120
Soup
- Beef Stew, 78
- Chicken Noodle soup, 46
- Chili, 74
- Classic Tomato Soup, 48
- Vegetable Beef Soup, 50

Spaghetti & Meatballs, 84
Sunday Dinner Chicken, 72
Taco Dinner, 76
Tex-Mex Seasonings, 26
Thousand Island Dressing, 20
Traditional Popcorn, 26
Vegetable Beef Soup, 50
Vegetables
- Glazed Carrots, 102
- Green Beans Almondine, 102
- Maple Butternut Squash, 100
- Mixed Veggies with Cheezy Sauce, 100

Waffles, 34
White Sandwich Bread, 106

# Notes

# Notes

Butter Flavor Crisco® as a registered trademark of Procter & Gamble Company, Cincinnati, OH; Coca-Cola® is a registered trademark of Coca-Cola Company, Atlanta, GA; Ener-G® is a registered trademark of Ener-G Foods, Inc., Seattle, WA; Fry Daddy® is a registered trademark of National Presto Industries, Inc., Eau Claire, WI; Ghirardelli® is a registered trademark of Chocoladefabriken Lindt & Sprüngli, Kilchberg, Switzerland; Haribo® is a registered trademark of GmbH & Co. KG. Bonn, GERMANY; Jelly Belly® is a registered trademark of Jelly Belly Candy Company, Fairfield, CA; Jones Soda® is a registered trademark of Jones Soda Co. (USA) Inc., Seattle, WA; Lea & Perrins®is a registered trademark of Promark Brands Inc., Meridian, ID; Sunbutter® is a registered trademark of Red River Commodities, Inc., Fargo, ND; Toastmaster® is a registered trademark of Toastmaster, Inc., Corporation Columbia, MO; Trolli® is a registered trademark of Trolli, Inc. Plantation, FL; Yummy Earth® is a registered trademark of YummyEarth LLC, Ridgewood, NJ.

Made in the USA
Lexington, KY
24 March 2010